SAVE the PLANET
The Aussie Kid's Guide
E
The Five Mile Press

The Five Mile Press Pty Ltd
950 Stud Road, Rowville
Victoria 3178 Australia
Email: publishing@fivemile.com.au
Website: www.fivemile.com.au

Illustrations by Ian Forss
Design and graphics by Canary Graphic Design
Edited by Niki Horin

First published 2008

The paper used to print this book is a natural product made from wood pulp grown in sustainable, well managed and certified plantation forests. The manufacturing processes used in the book's production conform to the environmental regulations in the country of origin.

Printed in China

National Library of Australia Cataloguing-in-Publication data:
Chapman, Helen, 1956- .
Save the planet: The Aussie kid's guide.

For primary school age.
ISBN 9781741789454 (pbk.).

1. Environmental protection - Citizen participation - Juvenile literature. 2. Human ecology - Juvenile literature. I. Forss, Ian. II. Title.
363.70525

Author acknowledgements: Dr Carolyn Polizzotto and Janette Leaver

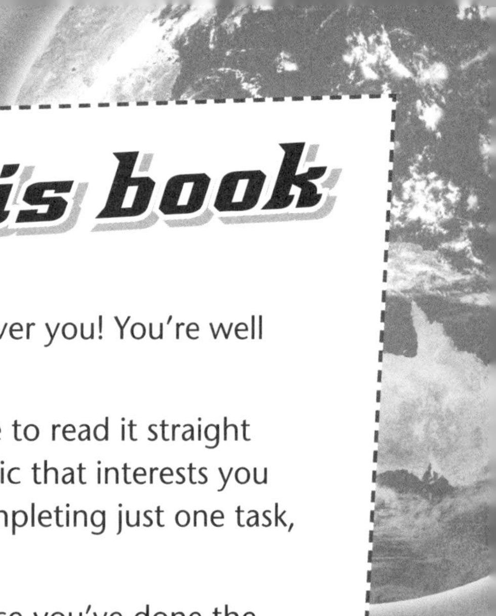

How to use this book

1. **Open it!** (But you've already done that. Clever you! You're well on the way to **making a difference.**)

2. **Start wherever you want.** You don't have to read it straight through from beginning to end. Pick the topic that interests you the most. Make that your first choice. By completing just one task, you'll help to **Save the Planet.**

3. **Read on.** Keep on reading! Once you've done the first project you'll be ready for the next.

4. Each topic has facts about the environment and more importantly it has me! I'm not just here for my good looks! My job is to challenge you to make a difference – whether you live in the city, suburbs or in the countryside. At home, at the shops, at school, out and about, on holiday – wherever you are, and whatever you're doing, **you can be a Superhero** too.

How to make a wriggly squiggly worm farm

by A.W.S. Worm

Kitchen scraps are poo-lluters of our planet

Do you know what happens to your kitchen scraps? They end up where all the rubbish ends up – at the tip. You'll never get rid of rubbish that way. Tips don't break down rubbish, they just bury it.

Kitchen scraps make greenhouse gas and pollute ground water.

In-sink garbage units send scraps to sewage treatment systems. This wastes water and uses chemicals.

Make your own worm farm!

Instead of throwing scraps away give them to us. Worms love scraps. We turn them into **poo**. Our poo fertilises plants and soil. And we help keep the environment clean.

MyHome Search

Home | Browse | Search | Invite | Film | Mail | Blog | Favourites | Forum | Groups | Music | Events |

Hey, welcome to my home! Come in and I'll show you around. It's easy to make your own worm farm!

My farm is made from: A polystyrene box (about 28 cm high) with lid, insect screen wire, and cardboard or newspaper.

The lid keeps inside cool and damp. Arghhh! Not the light! The birds will eat us – shut the lid!

The box has small pencil holes in the bottom. Holes let in oxygen and let out water. They also let out wee.

Eyk! Too much info!

My farm stands on bricks so the holes stay clear.

Insect screen wire sits in the bottom of the box. This wire stops us falling out.

Arrghhh splat!

My bed is made from:

My bed is made from damp, not wet, newspaper torn into strips.

Also, straw, grass and soil go well with scraps.

Deeeliiiciious!

If you're a worm, that is!

I have 999 friends. With me, that makes 1,000 of us! We came from garden nurseries or other worm farms. Don't forget to give us all names ... Good morning, Squishy!

Don't even think of buying my cousins the giant Gippsland earthworms. Not only are they a protected species, but also they grow up to three metres long. That's as long as a car! Where are you going to find a box for 1,000 of those?

My diet is made up of: ... kitchen scraps. Cooked food rots faster and we compost it faster. Raw food is good if it's been chopped or mashed.

Your farm jobs include:

- adding water to our box every few days. We die in dry soil, but also be careful not to drown us! We don't swim.
- adding kitchen scraps every week. The dog will be okay. It can eat canned food. We want all the scraps you've got.
- collecting the poo every few months. Who's the lucky boy or girl who has to do this job? It's called 'poop patrol'. It's okay. It's not as bad as cleaning up dog poo. Worm poo is tiny and doesn't smell.
- spreading our poo on the garden. It makes great compost. Also, try mixing it with potting mix to use on pot plants.

What about our babies?

We worms like to reproduce, so after six months the farm might have too many of us. What can you do? … No, we can't move in with you! So, build a second storey for us. Put scraps in the top box. We'll wriggle through the holes to reach them.

Or, to reduce our population in the box, you can put some of us in the garden.

Hey, the view is great from the top floor!

No! Don't put us in deep holes in the garden. That's **scary**. Just leave us on top with damp leaves and mulch.

MyHome Search

Home | Browse | Search | Invite | Film | Mail | Blog | Favourites | Forum | Groups | Music | Events |

My menu: good foods

Good foods for worms are:

- fruit, vegetables and peelings
- crushed cooked egg shells
- leftover cereal, bread, biscuit and cake crumbs
- soaked and ripped pizza boxes
- shredded wet cardboard and paper
- tissues
- dog poo (wait two weeks if the dog's been wormed)
- cat poo
- hair
- house dust
- used tea bags
- coffee grounds

MyHome Search

Home | Browse | Search | Invite | Film | Mail | Blog | Favourites | Forum | Groups | Music | Events |

My menu: bad foods

- citrus fruit and peel from mandarins, lemons, limes, oranges and grapefruit, pineapples, onions, leek and garlic
- dairy products, like milk, cheese and yoghurt
- fat
- oil
- meat, fish and bones

Continue the cycle: RECYCLE

Recycling means that materials stay in the loop and out of the tip. In the past nobody thought that recycling made a difference.

Can you believe it! Things that easily could have been reused or recycled were just thrown out.

Recycling is when you take materials from products you have finished using and make new products with them.

Go snooping! Wherever you go, look out for the recycle mark on products.

How many products can you find that have these logos?

Recycled

This symbol shows that something is made from material that has been used before. Unless it says otherwise, the product is 100% recycled.

Recyclable

This symbol shows that something *can* be recycled. It does not need to be made from recycled material.

First, look for paper towels, boxes or glass jars. Then see if you can find any surprises on the shelves.

Can you buy at least one thing made from recycled materials?
Less energy is used to make recycled products than new ones. You'll be helping the environment.

BECOME A SUPERMARKET SLEUTH

The average family throws out more than 4 kg of food packaging each week. Too much packaging is bad for the environment. It ends up as waste in the tip.

A **crime** is happening against everyday products. They're being smothered in too much paper, cardboard, plastic, shrink wrap and foam packaging.

How many over-packaged products can you find?

Look carefully at each product you and your family usually buy.

How is it packaged?

Does it have too much packaging?

If so, keep looking. Can you see the same type of product in less packaging? If not, is there a different way you can buy the product?

ARE YOU A SILLY SHOPPER ...

What's in your lunchbox?
Let's see how many smart packaging choices you can make.

shoppers buy
juice in tetra packs.

SMART **shoppers buy**
juice in a recyclable bottle.

Super tip: *At home pour the juice into a bottle or thermos.*

shoppers buy
chips and biscuits in single serve sizes.

SMART **shoppers buy**
chips and biscuits in big bags or packets.

Super tip: *At home put smaller servings into containers.*

OR A SMART SHOPPER?

SILLY shoppers buy

pre-made packaged puddings, desserts and yoghurts.

SMART shoppers buy

big tubs of yoghurt and instant puddings and dessert mixes.

Super tip: *At home you can quickly prepare the mixes and divide into tubs.*

SILLY shoppers buy

fruits and vegetables in foam trays and plastic wrap.

SMART shoppers buy

loose fruit and vegetables and put them into their own carry bag.

Super tip: *At home you can cut fruit into small bits and put into plastic tubs to make fruit cups.*

SILLY shoppers buy

pre-made packaged single lunch snacks.

SMART shoppers buy

local cheese, sandwich meat and crackers.

Super tip: *Before school make your own single lunch snack.*

Australia once had dinosaurs and FLESH EATING kangaroos. It even had crocodiles that jumped down on its prey from trees! They are now all extinct.
SAVE ENDANGERED – EAT A BILBY!
You kids eat chocolate versions of me at Easter – that's great. But don't forget that I am REAL! I need help. And I have equally endangered friends all around Australia!
Nooo, you're killing us ...
Going Going GONE
ENDANGERED

Help stop animals **going**, **going**, **gone** the way of the dinosaur … And to help the poor bilbies CHILL OUT!

Visit a wildlife sanctuary or a zoo. Your money goes towards food and care for the animals.

Sponsor an **endangered** species yourself, or organise for a group of friends, family or your school to sponsor a species. Many zoos have special breeding programs for wildlife in **danger**.

ENDANGERED

ENDANGERED

ENDANGERED

Feed the birds

Don't feed sugar, honey or jam to birds. These foods don't give birds the important nutrients they get from nectar. The birds fill up on sugars instead of nectar just like you do when you eat sweets instead of nutritious stuff.

Superhero Cheep-cheep Challenge

Make a birder feeder, and get the birds coming to your place.

You will need:

- plastic drink bottle
- string
- scissors
- chopsticks
- wild birdseed

- Waterproof acrylic paints and a paintbrush if you want to decorate your feeder
- Adult to help you with cutting the holes

Follow these steps:

1. Wash and dry the bottle.
2. Ask an adult to cut a hole in the side. Be careful to keep the edges smooth.
3. Under this hole cut two small holes on each side.
4. Slide a chopstick or rod through to make a perch. If you are going to decorate your feeder, this is the time to do it. Just make sure you leave enough time for paint to dry properly.
5. Make at least three small holes in the bottom to let rainwater drain out.
6. Add wild birdseed and tightly close the top.
7. Tie string under the lid. Knot it several times.
8. Hang your feeder from a balcony, veranda, tree branch or clothesline.
9. Keep the inside of the feeder clean. If it gets dirty, tip the seed out and wash the bottle with warm water and dry. IMPORTANT: a dirty feeder can give birds infections that can kill them.
10. If your feeder wears out, recycle it and make another one!

MESS UP THE GARDEN

Make your home a sanctuary for the local wildlife, and create a natural paradise while you're at it.

- Get into the garden and get messy. Make up a big and wide pile of leaf litter, mulch, twigs and small branches. Watch the pile over the next few weeks. Which insects, birds, mice, lizards or frogs visit your pile, or move in?

- Plant some native trees, shrubs and grasses. They give food to native wildlife over many months. Nectar and pollen, in particular, are food for many native birds, mammals and insects.
- Turn your lawn into a wildflower reserve! Plant some flowers and grasses. They will give food and shelter to native wildlife.

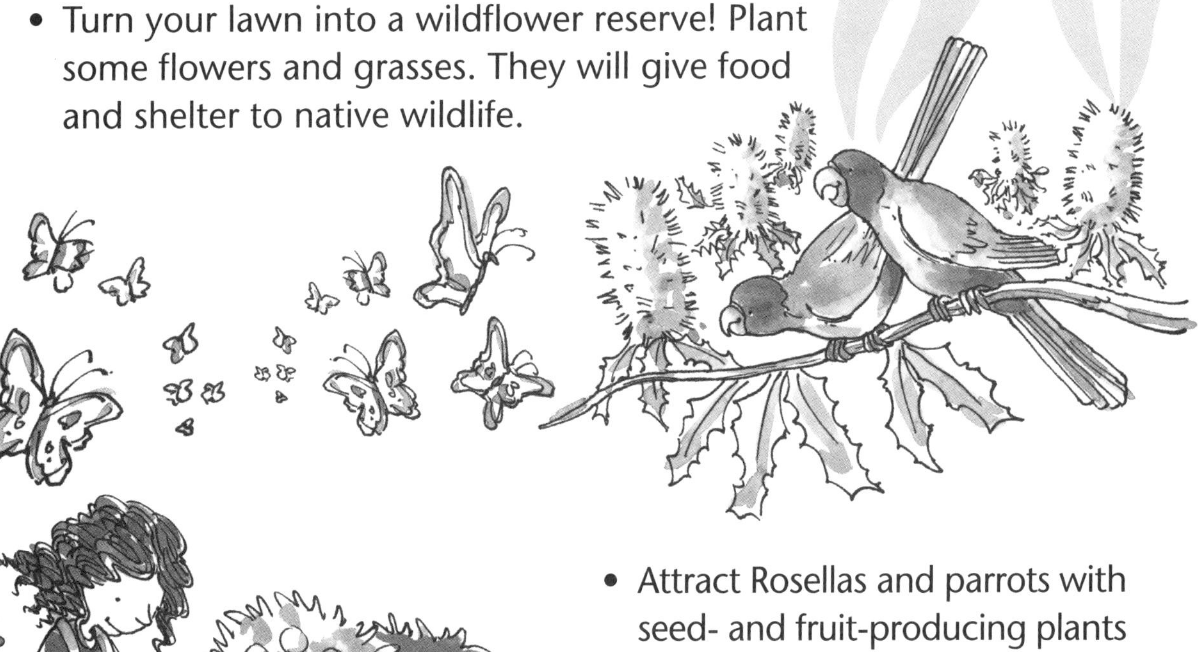

- Attract Rosellas and parrots with seed- and fruit-producing plants like grasses, wattles, casuarinas and eucalypts. Flying foxes, fruit bats and possums are attracted by fruit-bearing plants.
- And always remember to keep your cats inside at night.

HOW DO YOU MEASURE UP?

'Food kilometres' is a term used to measure the distance food travels from the fields, where the crops are grown or animals are reared, to your plate.

What are you having for dinner tonight? Has the food come from your local area? Or has it travelled a long way to get to your home?

Look in your fridge and kitchen cupboards.

Are there foods from other countries? You'll find the country where it is made by looking at the bottom of the label. Read the label carefully. If food has been 'packed in Australia from imported goods' this means the food is not local.

THE KILOMETRE CAFE

Milk from the countryside.

Eggs from the suburbs.

Set up a kilometre cafe at home and at the school fete.

Invite your friends around to your home cafe. How many items can you serve that have not had to travel a long way to be cooked and served?

Jam from the city.

At the next school fete set up this cafe. Why not have a competition among the parents who make food products for the cake and jam stalls? Which parent used ingredients that travelled the shortest distance to the fete?

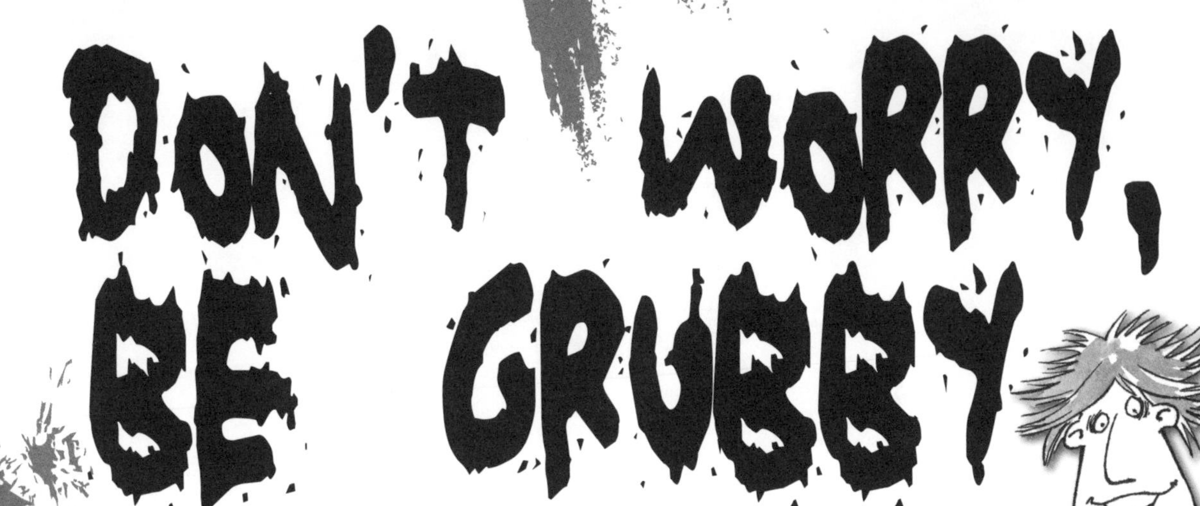

When you help do the washing it's best to use the washing machine when you've got a full load. A full load uses less water than two half loads.

SUPERHERO STORY TIME

Are you sitting comfortably? Then I'll begin. Once upon a time your great-grandmothers did the laundry once a week. Nowadays, it's usually done once a day – more if there's a baby in the house. The end.

How can you help to save water, energy and cut back on detergents? You can't do anything about the baby, but what about *your* clothes? Do they ever end up on the bedroom floor when you've only worn them once? And then you can't put them on again, because they've been on the floor – so straight into the laundry basket they go.

Superhero Grubby Challenge

Stop loading up the wash basket with cleanish clothes.

Save your favourite clothes for a second wear, or even a third if they aren't too grubby. Turn them inside-out so you know you've worn them before, or keep them in a special part of the wardrobe where you'll know they have already been worn ... Your favourite clothes will last longer and they won't always be waiting to be washed, so you'll be able to wear them when you want to!

THE PAPER THAT

Think about all the kinds of paper products that you use and throw out everyday. Egg cartons, newspapers, cereal boxes, envelopes, junk mail ... All of these items can be recycled and made into useful things.

But be careful, some things

NEVER DIE!

HOULDN'T DIE

Make your own seed paper.

You will need

- paper to recycle, such as egg cartons, paper bags, junk mail, tissue paper and/or old greeting cards
- egg beater and bowl, or blender/food processor (remember: mixing by hand saves energy)
- small, flat seeds from vegies or flowers, like cherry tomato, forget-me-not, hollyhock or chilli pepper

- strainer
- sponge
- bowl
- tea towel
- rolling pin
- adult to supervise, if using an electric blender or food processor

What to do

1. Tear recycled paper into small pieces.
2. Mix paper and warm water in a bowl, or half fill blender with pieces. Add warm water until blender is full. PUT LID ON SECURELY!
3. Blend until pulp is smooth.

4. Add seeds. Stir into pulp with a spoon.
5. Put strainer over a bowl and pour pulp through it. Squeeze out as much water as you can.
6. Tip pulp onto tea towel. Press flat with your hands or a rolling pin.
7. Shape into a sheet of seed paper. The size and thickness is up to you.
8. Press a dry sponge onto your seed paper to soak up any water.
9. Repeat steps 1 to 8 until you have all the sheets you want. Then dry the paper in a sunny spot.

What to do next

Use your seed paper to write on, or to wrap a gift.

For a gift, remember to include instructions on how to plant the paper:

PAPER PLANTING INSTRUCTIONS

1. To pre-sprout the seeds soak the seed paper until it's damp.
2. Tear off bits of seed paper.
3. Put good potting mix into a pot.
4. Add seed paper.
5. Sprinkle a little bit of potting mix on top.
6. Lightly water the seeds.
7. Put the pot in a sunny spot in the garden or inside.
8. Keep the soil damp and watch your seeds grow into seedlings.
9. Lift out the seedlings and plant in the garden.
10. Remember to keep the soil damp.

Note: In warm places the seed paper can go straight into a sunny spot in the garden.

DO YOURSELF A FAVOUR

There's not much fresh water. If 100 litres represents the world's water, then about half a tablespoon of it is fresh water.

Take the quiz!

You need to wash a few dirty dishes. Do you ...

1. Use the dishwasher?

2. Get your dog to lick them clean?

3. WASH THEM BY HAND? 

BE A WATER SAVER

You want a cold drink. Do you …

1. Run the tap and waste water running down the drain?

2. Yell 'MUM!!!'?

3. KEEP A JUG OF COLD WATER IN THE FRIDGE? ✔

You have vegetables to wash. Do you …

1. Put them back in the fridge and not bother?

2. Hold them under a running tap?

3. CLEAN THEM IN A BOWL OF WATER? ✔

You have boiled an egg. Do you …

1. SAVE THE COOLED WATER FOR YOUR POT PLANTS? ✔

2. Tip the water down the sink?

3. Give your goldfish a bath in the water?

I SEE THE LIGHT SURROUNDING YOU – SO SWITCH IT OFF!

In World War One soldiers in dark places put glow-worms into jars. They used these 'lights' to read maps!

Superhero Switch off Challenge

Keep your eye on the lights ... and switch off.

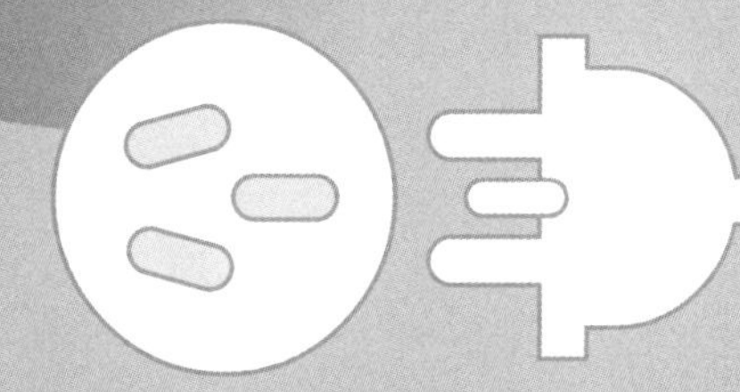

How often can you switch off a light when it doesn't have to be on? Once an hour? Once a day? Once a week?

Make up a chart and have a competition with your family or friends. Each time you turn off a light put a tick next to your name. Switch off and win!

But don't get too silly! All light bulbs use more energy to turn on than to burn for a while. So, if you are going out of the room for just a few minutes, leave the lights on.

Have you ever stopped a toddler from putting something dangerous into its mouth? Toddlers can't tell what is safe to eat and what isn't. Marine creatures such as whales, penguins, seals, dolphins, sea-turtles, sea birds and sea lions are just like toddlers!

They can't always tell what is safe to eat and what isn't. When they see plastic litter floating in the ocean they think it's food. Worldwide, around 1,000,000 seabirds and 100,000 marine mammals and turtles are killed by plastic litter every year.

If bits of litter get stuck in their throat, they choke. If bits of litter get stuck further down inside they block food from being digested and the creatures starve.

At the beach buy ice-cream in a cone, not in a foam or plastic cup ... and don't forget to throw your sticky napkin in the bin.

LEAVE ONLY

More than 143 types of marine life, including most turtle species, get caught in the litter we put into the ocean.

Litter not put in bins can end up in the ocean. Plastics are the most common litter found in the oceans. If marine life gets caught in plastic bags or plastic six-pack holders, they can starve to death or be strangled.

FOOTPRINTS

Superhero Scavenger Hunt Challenge

Clean up the beach.

Walk along the beach. Look at the sand dunes and peer into rock pools. See how much litter you and your friends can collect. Keep an eye out for plastic bags, plastic bottles and caps, plastic food and sweet wrappers, foam packaging from take-away food like hot chips and drinks, cans and glass bottles, icy-pole sticks and paper.

DO NOT touch sharp objects like broken glass and needles. Ask an adult to pick these up.

Without a garden ...

Easy peasy.

And without digging!

What? No way!

What you need

- 6–8 strawberry seedlings
- 1 bag of good potting mix
- recycled wooden or plastic tray or box to match the size of the bag
- gardening gloves
- watering can
- an adult to supervise

What to do

1. Choose a day that isn't windy. Or work in a sheltered spot. This is because it is not good to breathe in airborne potting mix.
2. Put on gloves.
3. Move the tray or box to where it will get the warm morning sun but not the hot afternoon sun.
4. Cut a few small holes into the underside of the bag. This lets water drain away.
5. Sprinkle water over the mix. This helps to stop you breathing in airborne particles.
6. Place bag in the box.
7. Cut 6–8 holes into the bag big enough to fit the roots of the seedlings.
8. Put a plant into each hole.
9. Put the bag into a tray or box. Use only one bag of potting mix for each tray so it can be moved easily.
10. Rinse gloves afterwards.
11. Always wash hands with soap and water after using potting mix.
12. Check your plants each day and water regularly.

HAY YOU!
Plants grown in hay need less water than plants grown in soil.
Superhero Tomato Challenge
Grow tomatoes ... without a garden ... and without digging!

WHAT YOU NEED

- gardening gloves
- bale of hay if you live in the country (or straw if you don't)
- a stick
- good quality potting mix
- 6–8 tomato seedlings
- watering can

WHAT TO DO

1. Put on your gloves.
2. Put bale somewhere where it will get sun for about 6 hours a day.
3. Put the bale on the ground so the string is around the sides rather than the top.
4. Jam a stick into the bale. Wiggle it around until you make a space for each seedling.
5. Fill the space with potting mix.
6. Place the tomato seedlings in the bale and water them.
7. As the seedlings grow the bale slowly breaks down. The roots go into the ground and the plants are already mulched!
8. Water as required.

THE HEAT IS ON

Heating is the single biggest use of energy in homes.

SUPERHERO STORY TIME

It's winter and it's cold. But does Carter care about saving energy? No, she doesn't!

If she feels cold she turns up the heating. Carter heats every room in the house even if the rooms are empty. She keeps the curtains and blinds open at night (so she can poke her tongue out at the boy next door). Carter leaves the heating turned up all night. She even leaves the heating on when she goes out. The End.

Don't be like Carter!

Put on warmer clothing when you're cold.

Close the door when a room is empty.

Close the curtains and blinds at night (and don't poke your tongue out at the boy next door).

Turn down the heating at night to 16 degrees Celsius or lower.

Turn the heating off when you go out.

ARE YOU CAR-LESS

ABOUT POLLUTION?

Record your family's car trips.

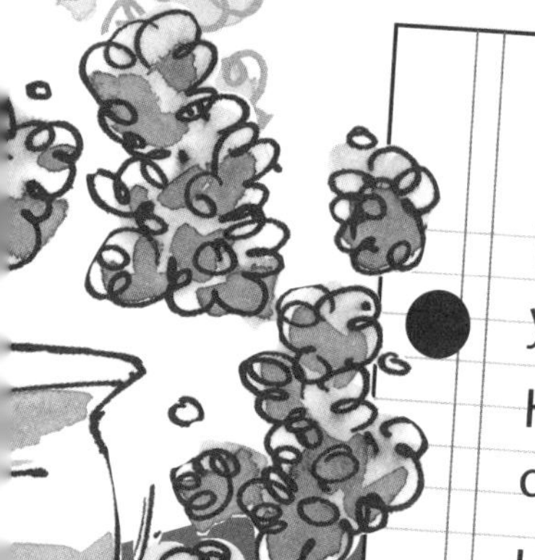

Make a list of all the car trips your family takes in a week. At the end of the week, look at the list. Think about the types of car trips that you and your family took.

How many trips could your family have done together?

How many trips could have been shared with friends to after-school activities and sport?

How many trips could have been done without the car?

Could you have walked? Ridden a bike? Used public transport?

THESE BOOTS ARE MADE FOR WALKING

Most of our oxygen was made by green plants within the last billion years. So, in fact, we don't make new air, we just recycle it. But then we go on dumping pollution into our air every day!

Most air pollution is caused by the things people do. When people drive cars and other vehicles, pollution is sent into the air. For every kilometre you and your family don't drive, the air is made that much healthier for you.

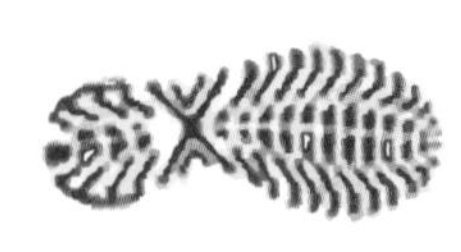

Walk or ride your bike to school and to visit friends.

Help set up a 'Walking Bus' to get to school. You need one adult up front as the 'driver' and another adult at the back. You walk to school and pick up other kids at 'bus stops' along the way. After school you do the opposite.

How far can one litre of fuel go?

A small car can carry one person for 9km on 1 litre of fuel

A bus with 40 passengers carries each person the equivalent of 50 km on 1 litre of fuel

A train carries each person the equivalent of 55km on 1 litre of fuel

WHAT'S LEFT OVER?

Over half of Australian homes don't recycle or reuse kitchen food.

Superhero Tasty Challenge

Make meat or vegetable fritters.

What you need

- 1 cup self-raising flour
- 1 egg
- 2 teaspoons of oil
- ¼ cup of water
- 1 onion, finely diced
- 2 cups of diced leftovers – meat or vegetables
- milk – any sort is fine, even soy
- olive oil for frying
- frypan
- adult to supervise the cooking

What to do

1. Put flour into a bowl. Make a hole in the centre.
2. Add egg, oil and water to the hole.
3. Gradually stir in flour.
4. Add milk slowly until your batter is smooth but thick.
5. Stir in onion and your choice of meat and/or vegetables. (There should be more meat and vegetables than batter.)
6. Spray or pour oil into a large frypan to cover the base.
7. Ask an adult to heat the oil.
8. Spoon fritters into oil as if you're making pikelets. Cook until golden brown on the bottom.
9. Turn fritters and cook on other side.
10. Drain on paper towels.
11. Serve hot.

WHAT'S LEFT OVER

Make Bubble and Squeak.

What you need

- lots of mashed potato, it makes up about two thirds of the ingredients!
- leftover cooked vegetables
- butter
- frypan
- adult to supervise the cooking

AND SQUEAKS?

What to do

1. Mix in any of the following leftovers with the potatoes – shredded cabbage, cauliflower, peas, broccoli, carrots, onion, mushrooms,etc.
2. Add flavourings like salt, pepper, herbs, or garlic if you want.
3. Put a knob of butter into a frypan.
4. Ask an adult to heat the pan.
5. Spoon the mix on top of the melted butter.
6. Flatten the mix to cover the bottom of the pan so it's about 2 ½ cm thick. Listen carefully – you might hear it squeak!
7. When the bottom has a golden brown crust, flip the Bubble and Squeak over and cook the other side until it is also crusty.
8. Drain on paper towels.
9. Serve hot.

WHAT'S LEFT OVER AND GOES WOOF OR MEOW?

When you adopt an animal from an animal shelter you help to reduce the number of unwanted animals in our community.

The RSPCA is the Royal Society for the Prevention of Cruelty to Animals. Each year in Australia they take in about 135,000 animals from people who can't look after their pets anymore. There are many other animal shelters too!

Superhero Pet Challenge

Visit your local animal shelter.

Next time your family is in search of a new pet, visit a shelter. Most shelters have kittens and cats, puppies and dogs. Others have different animals like rabbits, guinea pigs and even horses.

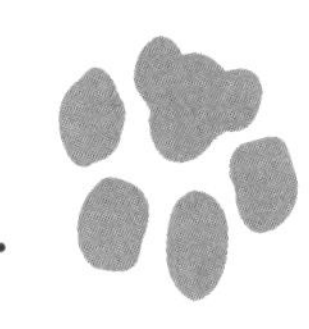

If you don't need a pet or can't have one at your place, you can help in other ways. You can donate a can of pet food. Animals are always hungry! Or look around the house for an old blanket and take it to the shelter. This can help to provide a lovely warm bed.

WHY DO SO MANY ANIMALS END UP IN SHELTERS?

The drought killed my grass. My owner couldn't afford to buy feed.

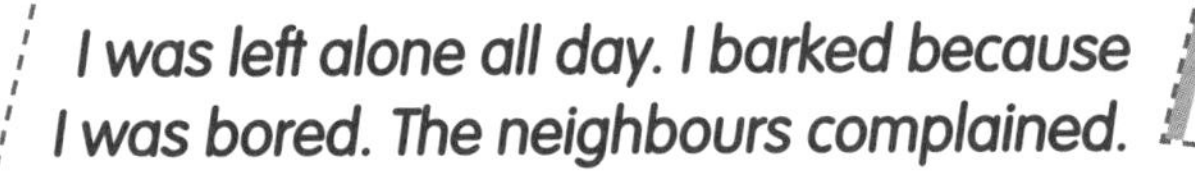

My owner got married. My fur made his wife sneeze! In the end it got so bad that she said it was her or me – so I am here!

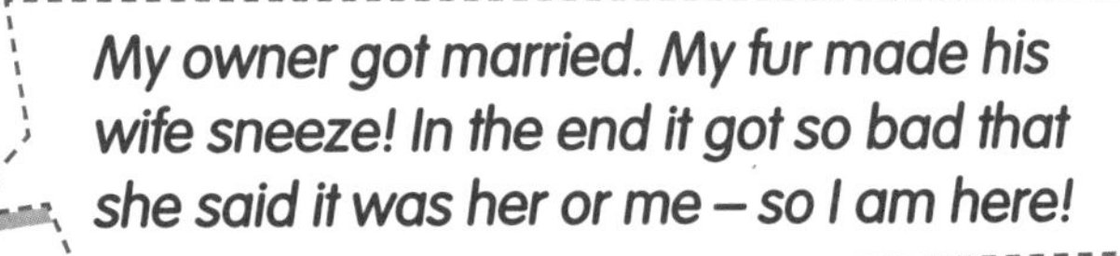

ARE YOU CRAFTY?

Making recycled gifts helps to reduce rubbish and keep the environment safe.

LOST

4 Remote Controls

Last seen somewhere in the family room.

Answers to the names of 'Have You Got', 'Where Is', 'You Had It Last' and 'Look under the Cat'

Make a recycled remote control holder.

WHAT YOU NEED

- an empty six-pack holder
- craft material, such as paper, stickers, labels, paint and coloured markers
- gluestick
- scissors

WHAT TO DO

1. Cover a six-pack holder with paper, contact or paint.
2. Decorate with stickers, drawings or cut out your own shapes to stick on.
3. When you find your remote controls put them in their new home.

RECYCLED SCHOOL PROJECTS

No! This doesn't mean you do one project then keep using it every year!

What happens when you have to do a school project? Do you go out and buy new craft materials? Well, not any more!

Make all your school projects from recycled materials.

Before you put items into the recycle bin see if they'd be good for projects. Start saving anything you think you will need. If you need a box use one from home, or most supermarkets have heaps of boxes for you to take.

Talk with your teachers. They might ask their classes to use only recycled materials too.

Much of the energy used in the kitchen is for cooking.

Not all biscuits and sweet snacks need to be put in an oven. When you are leafing through recipe books, look for sweet slices which say 'no bake' or for biscuits called 'refrigerator cookies'. Hedgehog Slice is one delicious example.

No, it's not! It tastes awful. Try Rat Slice instead.

(Author disclaimer: No hedgehog was harmed in the making of this recipe!)

What you need

- bowl
- big spoon
- 18 x 28 cm shallow pan, like a roasting dish but smaller.
- saucepan
- 3 tablespoons sugar
- 1 ½ tablespoon milk
- 1 ½ tablespoon cocoa
- 2 teaspoons vanilla essence
- 125 g butter
- 1 egg
- 250 g broken plain sweet biscuits
- baking paper
- adult to supervise the cooking stage in the 'no cook' recipe

What to do

1. Line the pan with baking paper. This stops the mix sticking to the pan.
2. Put the sugar, milk, cocoa, vanilla essence and butter into a saucepan.
3. Ask an adult to put the saucepan on the stove over low heat and bring mix to the boil.
4. Ask an adult to remove the saucepan from the heat as soon as the mix starts to boil.
5. When the mix is lukewarm tip it into a bowl.

6. Beat in the egg with a spoon.
7. Stir in the broken biscuits.
8. If you like fruit or nuts add ¾ cup of chopped sultanas, currants or walnuts.
9. Tip the mix into the pan and gently press flat.
10. Put in the fridge until set, which will take about one hour.
11. Take set mix out of the fridge. Let it come to room temperature before icing.
12. Ice if you want to and then cut into squares.

To make the icing you will need

- 1 cup icing sugar
- 1 tablespoon cocoa
- 1–2 tablespoons hot water
- Small bowl
- Spoon
- Flour sifter

Sift the icing sugar and the cocoa into a bowl. Add the hot water. Mix to a smooth paste. Spread the icing evenly over the slice and set. You can also sprinkle some desiccated coconut or chocolate sprinkles on top to make the slice look like a hedgehog!

WIPE OUT

Charity shops re-use some goods and recycle many others. Check out your local op shop! They stock heaps of great things and make a big contribution to caring for the environment.

In a charity shop you can find clothing, toys, books, games, vases, ornaments and CDs. However, over one-third of goods donated to charity shops can't be used. They can't sell torn clothes or anything broken and not working. These end up dumped in the tip. This costs the charity many thousands of dollars as they must pay workers, transport costs and tip fees.

Find one good quality item to take to a charity shop.

If you find tatty old clothes, cut them up and put in the rag bag. Rags are better than paper towels and they can be used around the home, washed and used again.

If you find any broken goods, put them in recycle bins.

Remember to check with your family before you give anything away!

SWAP IT AT A SWAP SHOP

Be brave! Peek in your wardrobe. Is it bursting with old clothes and toys? You know, the favourite jeans that you've grown out of. The stuffed toy you don't love anymore. Or the babyish t-shirt your Gran gave you that you only wear when she comes to visit.

You can share, swap and recycle things you don't want in return for things you do. It's fun seeing your favourite things getting a new life. And who knows, the babyish t-shirt may become someone else's favourite piece of clothing!

WHAT TO DO

1. Make sure everything is clean and in good condition.
2. Set up a table or a groundsheet outside.
3. Put books, DVDs, CDs and computer games in shallow boxes so friends can flip through them.
4. Hang clothing from a clothesline or stack neatly in a pile.
5. Have fun swapping! Anything left over can go to a charity.

IS THERE FUZZ IN YOUR FRIDGE?

The biggest user of electricity on a daily basis is the fridge.

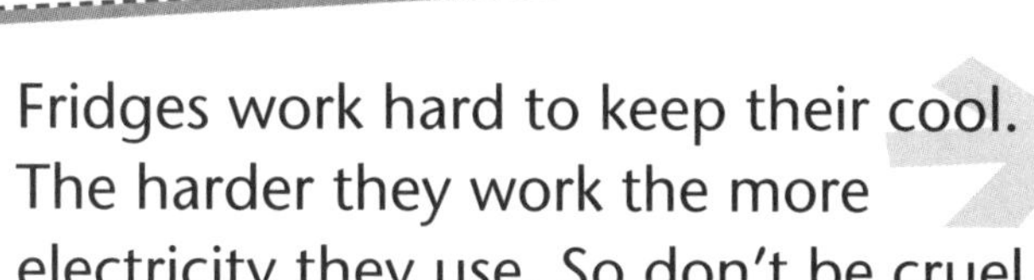

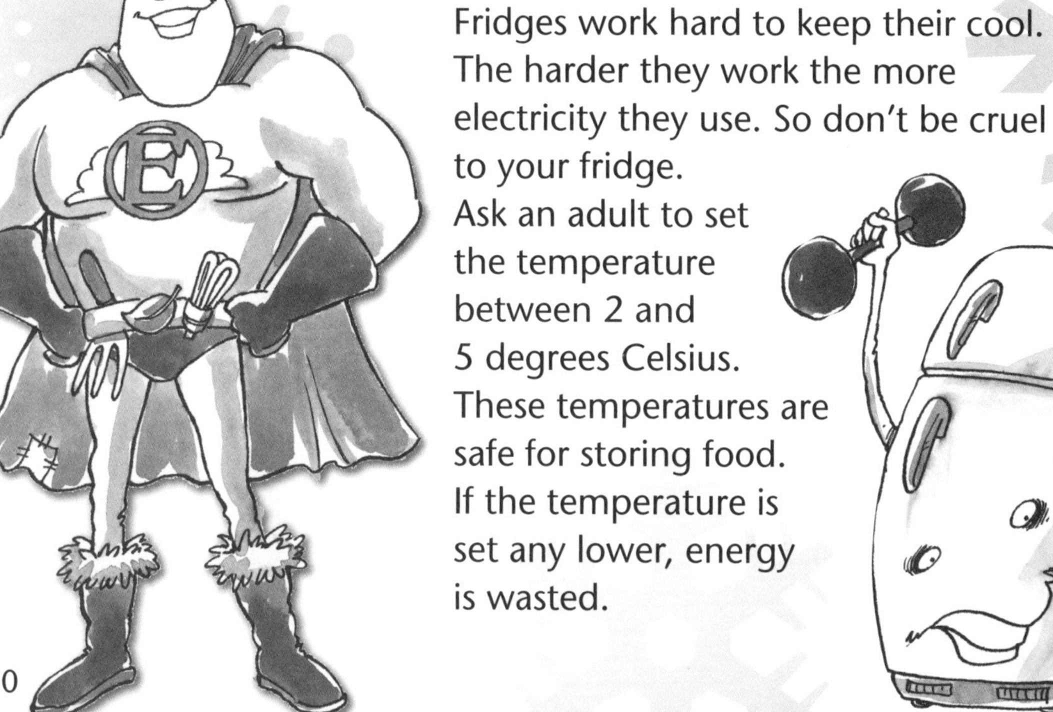

Fridges work hard to keep their cool. The harder they work the more electricity they use. So don't be cruel to your fridge.

Ask an adult to set the temperature between 2 and 5 degrees Celsius. These temperatures are safe for storing food. If the temperature is set any lower, energy is wasted.

How fast can you get food or drink out of your fridge? When you go to the fridge don't open the door and then work out what you want. That will just heat up the fridge and waste energy. Know what you want before you open the door. Remove the food or drink as fast as you can and quickly shut the door.

DON'T LOVE WILDLIFE TO DEATH

As more people visit wilderness areas, more rubbish is left behind. This hurts the animals and pollutes the environment.

Stop trying to fatten me up – I'm not Hansel or Gretel. Seriously, I'm meant to be skinny. I'm a hunter but you've turned me into a stalker. Instead of kangaroos and sheep I now eat picnic food and scraps. Bad, bad tourists – you don't obey the rules about not feeding me, and you get up close to take photos. I know my looks are to die for but being friendly will get people killed. I hang around campsites now and will stalk then attack you. I'm not mean, I'm just wild. But it's so unfair. If I hurt you I get put down.

Leave the campsite cleaner than you found it by cleaning up any litter that you see.

Don't feed any wildlife. It causes animals to lose their fear of people. When this happens they can become dangerous. Also, our food can make them very sick.

BE ENERGETIC

Go gadget free – and put your appliances into early retirement.

Make cake batter with a wooden spoon and mixing bowl.

Make a smoothie by mashing soft fruit in a jug then use a hand beater.

Make orange juice by using a lemon squeezer or reamer.

Knead bread by hand.

For small meals, the microwave oven is often the best and most eco-friendly way of cooking.

When something has an 'on-standby' setting it increases the use of electricity. But microwave ovens are a bit different.

Microwave ovens use a lot of energy. Is that right? Yes, but only if they are on for a long time.

In most cases, microwaves heat food so quickly that they end up using about half the energy of a standard oven. Microwaves are good to use in hot weather. They make less heat and this means less energy is wasted on having to cool the kitchen.

Use a microwave to warm up or cook small amounts of food instead of using the oven.

Are you allowed to use the microwave oven? If not, maybe you could suggest to whoever is doing the cooking that they use the microwave whenever possible.

For big meals, however, the stove is often better, especially if its energy comes from gas.

Ask your parents if your kitchen has a gas or electric stovetop and gas or electric oven.

How many kids does it take to change a light bulb?

None.
Kids are smart! They use compact fluorescent bulbs that last for ages.

Screw in a Light BULB

Compact fluorescent light bulbs last 10 times longer than regular bulbs and use 75 per cent less energy. Tubes are even better! Fluorescent tubes use 60–80 per cent less energy than bulbs and last up to 20 times longer.

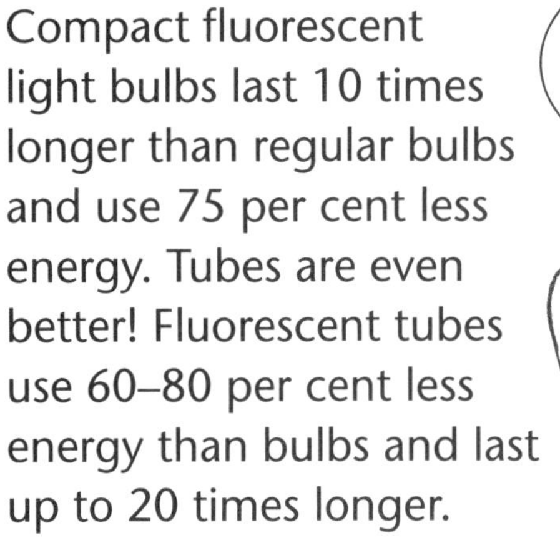

Superhero Fluoro Challenge

Keep an eye on the lights.

Walk around the house when it's dark. Which lights do you use the most? Are they fluoro? If not, talk to your parents. Ask if the lights that you use the most can be changed to fluoro.

Even by changing just one light to fluoro you can reduce energy and pollution.

Is the food being cooked on a stove? If so, does the pan completely cover the burner? It's important that it does. This heats the pan and food far better than a small pan on a big burner.

Are the lids on the pans? They should be. Lids help to stop the heat from escaping.

A COOK NUTS

Stop! Don't let anyone pre-heat the oven. It wastes energy and is not necessary for roasts or other meat dishes as the food starts cooking while the oven heats up. Preheat your oven only for cakes, biscuits and other foods that have baking powder.

Don't open the oven door to peek inside as heat escapes. The oven then has to waste energy heating up again.

Put Your Computer to Sleep

Every year, we use more energy than we did the year before. One reason for this is that even when they are not in use many appliances still use electricity for things like their stand-by control, clock and remote control.

Energy is there whenever we need it, so it's easy to forget where it comes from. A lot of it is wasted by using too much or not using it carefully. All of that energy adds up.

Superhero Sleepy Challenge

Put your computer to sleep when you're not using it.

A computer's standby power use can equal a 75 or 100 watt light bulb running continuously, so turn **off** the computer at night.

Turn off the TV, VCR, DVD, CD players and radio if no-one is using them. Check if it's okay with your parents, but the best thing is to **turn everything off** at the surge protector.

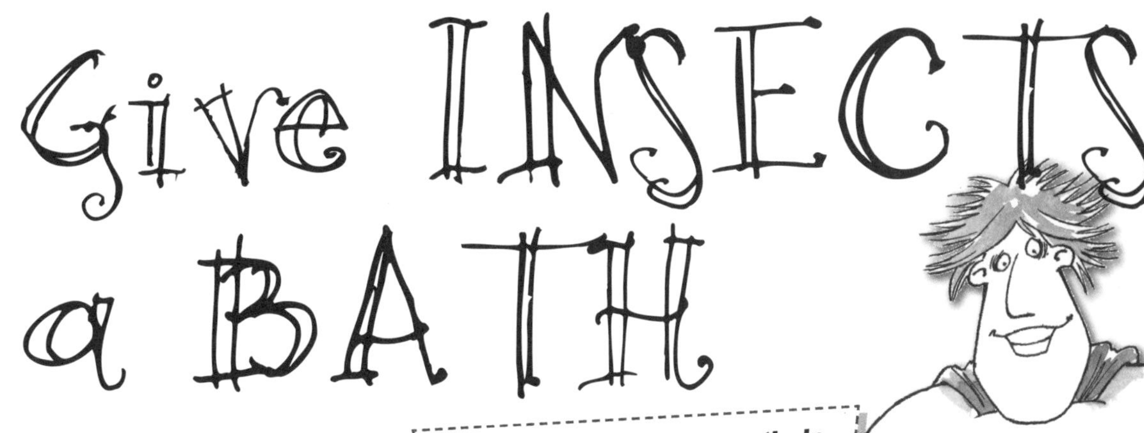

Insects may be small, but when there is a drought, they suffer too.

Insects get water from their prey or from plant sap, but mostly they get it from raindrops or dew.

Make an insect bath.

What you need

- small birdbath or shallow dish
- gravel or pebbles
- small rocks
- watering can

1. Put the gravel, pebbles and rocks in the birdbath.
2. Build them up to make little islands. Insects can land on these and can drink without drowning.
3. Use a watering can to fill up the bath.
4. You don't need to search for insects. They are delicate and easily harmed by touching. It's better to be patient and let them come to the bath.
5. Top up the water when needed.

WEATHER MAP YOUR HOME

Stop energy leaks around the home.

1. Make a map of your home. On the map draw windows, doors that lead outside and doors that lead to a garage or any unheated areas.
2. Walk around your home with a ribbon or strip of paper. Hold it up to the edges of the doors and windows. If the ribbon moves, you've found a leak!
3. Mark leaks on your map.
4. Show the map to your family and ask them to seal the leaks around your home.

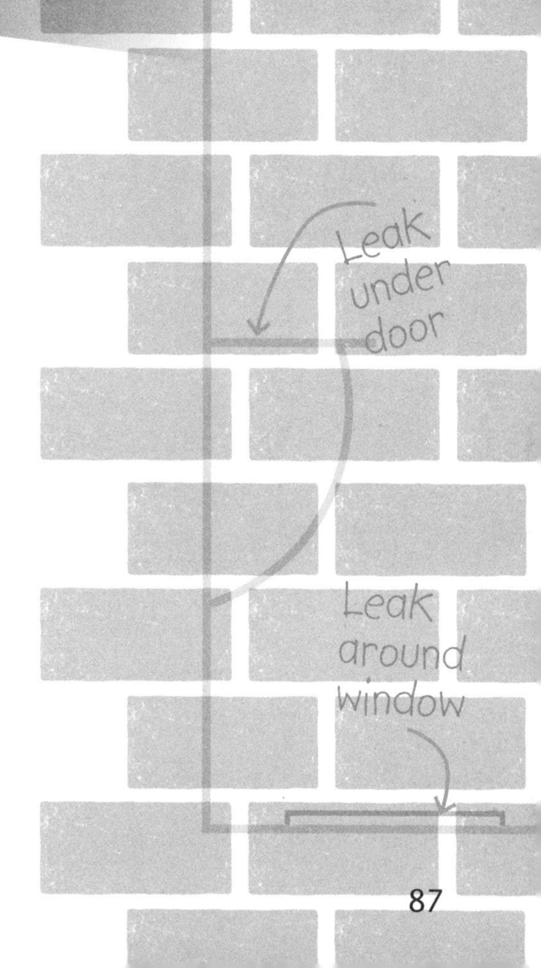

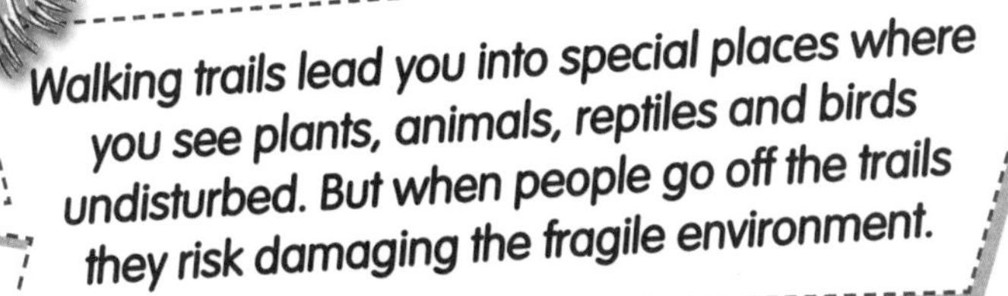

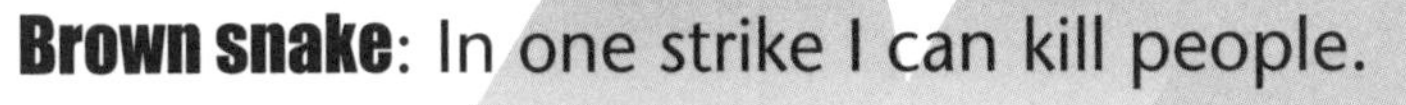

Brown snake: In one strike I can kill people.

Koala: *I can pee on them.*

Brown snake: That'll work.

Koala: *You don't actually go out and attack people do you?*

Brown snake: No … there's not much point – I can't eat them. But I'll strike if they tread on me or pick me up. I ask you, do I look like firewood?

Koala: *You're long and brown and a bit thick – so yes, actually!*

Stay on trails or dirt roads to avoid disturbing the wildlife.

Don't make short cuts across bushland, scrub, sand dunes and through forests.

Be careful walking around. Don't pick wildflowers, native fruits or berries.

Enjoy looking at our wonderful wildlife.

Take photographs to remind you of these beautiful creatures. But don't try to get too close and **DON'T TOUCH!**

Get into the GREEN SCENE

The earth has lost 30% of its natural habitat in the past 30 years. Tourism often makes life worse for wildlife and natural landscapes, but not if you choose an eco-friendly holiday.

Go on tours and activities that support the local community, wildlife and habitat.

Buy souvenirs that are made and sold by local people. Be careful not to buy anything made from endangered species, or that have animal skins or parts made of shells, tortoise-shell, ivory or coral.

Use public transport. In some countries you'll see more than buses, trams and trains. Try to ride in a rickshaw, ox-cart, camel, donkey or horse-drawn carriage. All of these are about as environmentally friendly as you can get. Not only do you help the local businesses, but also you get to experience something different.

MESSAGE IN A BOTTLE

Most plastic bottles are not being recycled. They litter the environment and fill tips.

Make your own brand of bottled water.

You will need

- plastic water bottles
- sticky address labels, or paper and glue
- scissors
- pencils or markers to decorate

What to do

1. Clean the bottles inside and out. They must be spotless.
2. Work out a clever name and logo for your bottled water. Draw this onto the sticky labels or cut paper into labels.
3. Stick or glue a label onto each bottle.
4. Give them to friends and family. Next time they want to take bottled water with them, they fill the bottle with tap water.
5. Remind everyone to recycle the bottle for next time.

Shower with an Egg Timer...

The bathroom is where most of the water in your home is used, so it is the place where you can save the most.

Baths use 200 litres of water. A shower with a standard head uses 17 litres every minute and a shower with a low water flow head uses only 7 litres every minute.

Save water showering and brushing your teeth.

What to do

1. Keep an egg timer in the bathroom.
2. Before each shower, turn on the timer.
3. See if you can get your shower down to three minutes, and still get clean!
4. Time each member of your family. Who has the fastest time?

Brushing your teeth with the tap running wastes water. But don't stop brushing your teeth! Wet your toothbrush then rinse out from a glass of water.

I save the planet by recycling my jokes!